Luis de Rivera

A UNIFIED THEORY OF WORK PLACE HARASSMENT

PSYCHODYNAMICS OF MOBBING

Instituto de
Psicoterapia
de Madrid

A Unified Theory of Work Place Harassment
The Psychodynamics of mobbing

Copyright 2012 © Luis de Rivera
www.luisderivera.com

© de esta edición, Instituto de Psicoterapia
de Madrid, 2012

Avenida de Filipinas 52
28003 Madrid .
tel. 91 534 5664
www.psicoter.es

Interior design: Richard Metcalfe

Special large print edition

ISBN-10: 1478205253

ISBN-13: 978-1478205258

Otras obras por Luis de Rivera:

El Maltrato Psicológico
Síndromes de Estrés
Medicina Psicosomática
Listado Breve de Síntomas – LSB 50
Cuestionario de Estrategias de Acoso – LIPT 60
Índice de Reactividad al Estrés
Las Claves del Mobbing

www.psicoter.es

CONTENTS

INDEX OF TABLES

A UNIFIED THEORY OF WORK PLACE HARASSMENT

PSYCHODYNAMICS OF MOBBING

THE PROBLEM

Work place harassment is referred to as "adult bullying" in the U.K. and in the U.S.A. and as "mobbing" in the European mainland. Although many authors tend to use both terms interchangeably, there is a fine distinction to be made: *Bullying,* the adult version of school harassment, implies the action of a *bully*, an agent more powerful than the victim, who may act alone or with willing accomplices. *Bossing* is a specific instance of bullying, in which the direct superior is the bully.

Mobbing is a collective activity, in which the harassment is sustained by peers and even inferiors. *Institutional harassment* is a specific instance of mobbing, in which the whole of the

1

organization gangs up on or shuns a target.

If we follow this terminology, bullying seems to be more prevalent in individualistic cultures or subcultures, while mobbing is so in more socialistic ones (Westhues, 2004). Other terms have been suggested, such as Workplace Bullying (Quine, 1999), Workplace Mobbing (Westhues, 2004), Psychological Terrorization at Work (Leymann, 2000), and even Counterproductive Work Behavior (Fox and Spector, 2005).

In any event, I recommend the use of the wider term Workplace Harassment (WPH) when no clear, specific distinction among nuances is made. It is not only in an attempt to unify terminology that I use this term, but also as a tribute to Carroll M.

Brodsky (1976), the author of "The harassed Worker", the first psychiatric study on the subject.

The study and prevention of WPH has been declared a priority in the European Union, where it is estimated to affect seriously at least 12% of workers (European Foundation for the Improvement of Working and Living Conditions, 2005). Health-care workers seem to be at increased risk, and alarms have been sounded to further investigate the problem (Cusack, 2000). According to a survey in a National Health Service community trust in England, 38% of employees report suffering one or more types of bullying in the previous year (Quine, 1999). Life-time prevalence in the U.K. has been estimated as 50 % (McAvoy, 2003). Harassed workers show higher scores of depression, anxiety, and stress than non-harassed workers (Quine, 1999), as well as irritability, increased arousal, sleep difficulties and nightmares, difficulty in concentration, work-related obsessions, the phobic avoidance of the work place and of job issues (Leymann, 1996; Mikkelsen, 2002) and "focalized thought pressure" or need to talk about work difficulties even if the context is inappropriate (de Rivera, 2002).

More data on the psychopathological effects of Work Place Harassment is offered in the Apendix (page 99)

SYMPTOMS OF MOBBING

- FOCALIZED THOUGT PRESSURE
- CONCENTRATION DIFFICULTIES
- OBSSESIONAL INTRUSIONS
- RECURRENT DREAMS
- DIFFICULTY RISING IN THE MORNING
- PHOBIC AVOIDANCE OF WORK PLACE
- ANXIETY - DEPRESSION
- PSYCHOSOMATIC SYMPTOMS

Source: Luis de Rivera 2002

EVOLUTION OF MOBBING

- REACTION = RECOVERY
- DEVELOPMENT = CRONIFICATION
  - ➤ HOSTIL-PARANOIDE
  - ➤ DEPRESSIVE
  - ➤ PSYCHOSOMATIC
  - ➤ MIXED
- CREATIVE SUBLIMATION

Source: Luis de Rivera 2002

DEFINITION OF WPH

An operational definition of workplace harassment has to exclude occasional instances of confrontation, conflict, hardship, or rudeness, as well as the stress produced by demanding or difficult occupations. All of those situations may be causes of work stress in their own right, but they are neither bullying nor mobbing.

4 TYPES OF WORK STRESS

- SIMPLE
- TRAUMATIC
- BURN-OUT
- MOBBING

WPH is a psychosocial disorder produced by the abusive interaction of a bully or bullies and a target, in an environment that tolerates or cooperates with this abuse. According to my proposal (Rivera, 2005), a given experience has to meet five criteria to be defined as mobbing: unfair psychological pressure or mistreatment occurs; the mistreatment is frequent, persistent and repetitive; the victim lacks the possibility of escape or defense; the abuse takes place in an unsympathetic environment; the aim is to eliminate the victimized worker or destroy his health and abilities.

We may find mobbing dynamics going on in all kinds of social groups (schools, families, condominium properties, etc). All forms of abuse, harassment, aggression and violence are characterized by an asymmetrical power relationship, in which one party harms and the other is harmed. In the case of psychological harassment an additional element exits: a humiliating sense of domination that gradually wears down the victim's human condition.

WPH does not consist in a sudden aggressive outburst, or in the application of an ambiguous paternalistic affection, not even in the isolated affirmation of a desire for power. Rather, it is as a persistent attitude of cold, deliberate and destructive control.

Even in these terms, the asymmetrical and abusive interaction between aggressor and victim is not enough. A third ingredient

9

is necessary, one which stems from the sociocultural group to which they both belong. In order for a chronic situation of psychological harassment at the workplace to be maintained, it is necessary that the social environment participates as an accomplice, a contributor or at least a consenting bystander.

As all abusers know, a certain level of isolation facilitates the abuse, by limiting the escape routes of the victim and preventing the intrusion of help.

This isolation effect is especially evident in cases of child abuse, couple abuse and elder abuse. In WPH isolation is more subtle, and the abuser has to reduce the scope of the social environment by means of secrets and lies, since the more people are aware of what is going on, the greater the probability that someone will try to put a stop to it. But let's not be too confident in human courage and altruism: History shows that large groups, social classes and even whole nations have consented and encouraged the vilest situations of abuse.

THE FIVE CRITERIA OF MOBBING

1. Psychological mistreatment or unfair or excessive pressure
2. Frequent, repeated, persistent
3. Neither escape nor defense possible
4. Encouraged or tolerated by the social group
5. Aimed to eliminate the target or to destroy his/her health and capacity

---

Source: Luis de Rivera 2002

THE DYNAMICS OF WPH

Psychological harassment, in all of its varieties, is a complex psychosocial syndrome generated by an interaction of dynamics created by the abuser, the victim and the psychosocial group to which they both belong. All three factors are necessary, and none of them, by itself, is sufficient. Together, these dynamics of abuse are activated and reactivated in a cyclical manner, crystallizing into a stable system - a vicious cycle whose duration and consequences depend on the strength and good fortune of the victim.

PSYCHOSOCIAL FACTORS OF WPH

depending on the abuser

☐ Mediocrity

☐ Envy

☐ Control

depending on the victim

☐ Authenticity

☐ Naivety

☐ Affective dependence

Depending on the social environment

☐ Isolation

☐ Cohesion

☐ Lack of productivity

I- **Factors that depend on the abuser**

In order for the harassment to take place, particularly in its institutional form, it is necessary for a person to assume the role of main persecutor. Not everybody is fit for this role; in the first place, he or she must be invested with sufficient authority or charisma to mobilize the persecutory dynamics of the group; and second, he must be endowed with some personality traits that make the persecutory role not only easy, but even an enjoyable one.

The personality of abusers has been described as displaying a peculiar combination of narcissistic and paranoid features, which allows them to convince themselves and others of the reasonable and just nature of their destructive acts. As all character disorders, they are unable to perceive their abnormality. Marie-France Hirigoyen (1998) considers this to be an asexual form of perversion; Tim Field (1996) describes it as a form of aggressive sociopathy; Scott Peck (1983) describes it as a "malign personality"; and Luis de Rivera (1997) describes it as "Active inoperative mediocrity disorder" or "*AIM syndrome*".

THE AIM SYNDROME

The AIM Syndrome is a character disorder often found in institutional bullies, First described in 1997, It has been confirmed over the years by many independent observations.

The main defining features of the Disorder by Active Inoperative Mediocrity or AIM syndrome are:

A - Evil Mediocrity

B − Malignant Envy

C - Need for control.

We shall describe those features in the following pages.

A) MEDIOCRITY

Following Maslow (1954), I contend that normal human nature tends towards excellence. The pursuit of excellence may be direct, through personal betterment, or indirect through identification or association with admired persons. The "pressure towards excellence" is an internal tension that seeks discharge either directly, by active efforts to personal improvement, or vicariously by passively admiring other people or actively fostering and aiding in their progress. Mediocrity is the lack of this capacity, like short-sightedness is a lack of visual acuity or cowardice is a defect of the capacity to face danger.

According to this view, mediocrity

has to be differentiated from objective achievements, and from the opinions of oneself or others regarding personal success. Indeed, an excessive "pressure towards excellence" generates a pervasive feeling of dissatisfaction that leads many extraordinary people to feel like failures, while mediocre individuals, who lack this internal pressure, usually feel quite happy with themselves.

In summary, I define mediocrity as the lack of interest, appreciation or aspiration towards excellence. According to its severity and intensity, three levels of mediocrity can be identified, known colloquially as the empty, the fatuous and the evil.

THREE TYPES OF MEDIOCRITY

I: Simple mediocrity. The Empty

II: Pseudo-creative mediocrity. The Fatuous

Type III: The AIM Syndrome. Evil mediocrity

Type 1: Simple mediocrity. The Empty

This is the least severe form of mediocrity. Often, it can be passed by unnoticed. In fact, people of this type may appear to the casual observer as exponents of the most perfect normality. Its two main symptoms are hyper-adaptation to current standards and lack of originality. Both features lead to conformity, and in many types of society, conformity leads to happiness

.

The simple mediocre is incapable of all creativity, but may follow paths well-trodden, tends to be a good consumer, adapts well to the materialist culture in which we live and, with a little instruction, can reproduce in his conduct a superficial display of artistic and scientific activities.

In contrast with the rebelliousness and the lack of social adaptation that sometimes appears as a pathological expression of the pressure towards excellence, the simple mediocre individual is a "normopath", whose illness consists in an excessive sociocultural adaptation; or, in other words, is incapable of developing an autonomous, independent personal life. The total lack of psychic creativity leaves the simple mediocre person totally helpless in face of the experience of human finiteness (hence the nickname "empty"). Therefore, any existential questions (which are rarely considered by him, anyway) throw him into a fit of anxiety. The internal emptiness of the normopath tends to be filled with external rules and events, converting him into a faithful follower of any well-delineated movement, whether religious, political or cultural.

Type II: Pseudo-creative mediocrity. The Fatuous

This is a somewhat more severe disorder, one who is liable to create unnecessary suffering and difficulties.

While the simple mediocre individual follows with ease the standard guidelines of prevalent behavior, without making any effort beyond the strict minimum required, in the pseudo-creative mediocre individual craving of distinction and flashes of competition and passive-aggressive opposition to the leaders begin to emerge. He is uncomfortable with the empty anonymous simplicity, and develops a tendency to imitate the creative processes of excellent individuals. Creativity, understood as the "*manifestation of the constructs of the internal world in the external world*" (de Rivera, 1993), is a major sign of the pressure towards excellence, and that is something mediocre individuals completely lack. However, in the pseudocreative subtype has a strong wish to appear to be excellent, which he tries to satisfy by imitation, hence his name. At difference with the simple-mediocre individual, who had no interest for prominent or managerial roles, the pseudocreative individual feels the need to appear to be important. For this reason, he is attracted to leadership positions, not so much because of the achievements and developments he may contribute to from these positions, but due to the image they confer. As he sees everything in the same way, unable to distinguish between beauty and ugliness, good and bad, sterility and creativity, the pseudocreative individual does not feel inclinations to facilitate any type of progress, and everything he is involved in is doomed to stagnation.

As it is true for character disorders in general, the people who interact with the pseudocreative-mediocre individual suffer more than the individual himself, as he tends to feel quite satisfied in his fatuous pseudocreativity. As a leader, he tends to produce and stimulate repetitive and imitative maneuvers, is more given to consensus than to discovery, and always prefers well-trodden methods to innovative approaches. In most cases, his pathology has limited repercussions, unless he reaches a key position of great responsibility. On this case, the organization that suffers him soon begins to display growing signs of functional paralysis, generally accompanied by a bureaucratic hyperactivity that attempts to disguise the lack of effectiveness.

Type III: The AIM Syndrome. Evil mediocrity

Technically referred to as "disorder by active-inoperative mediocrity", the AIM syndrome is a very malign variant of mediocrity, both because its direct deleterious effects and for its dangerous invasive tendencies. It tends to overlap somewhat with the previous type, but serious cases are clearly identifiable. The mediocrity of all serious abusers and harassers belongs to this category.

Typically, the individual affected by AIM syndrome is tenacious, even hardworking, displays a great deal of ineffective activity and has a great desire for fame and influence. AIM- individuals tend to infiltrate complex organizations, particularly those already affected by lesser forms of mediocrity. They easily dominate small groups that produce nothing but carry out "monitoring and control" functions, which allow the AIM individual to hinder the advance of brilliant people.

Within academic circles, which incidentally are quite susceptible to infection by the AIM syndrome, the affected individual pretends the pose of a master, falsifying his own merits and unscrupulously arrogating to himself those of others. If he has bureaucratic power, he introduces all sorts of regulations and procedures and generates large amounts of unnecessary paper-work that he actively imposes on others, so as to destroy their useful time and to hinder their truly creative abilities. While in the lesser forms of mediocrity there is simple incapacity to value excellence, the AIM-type individual tries to destroy it with every means at their disposal, developing sophisticated systems of hindrance and persecution. He will never recognize the merits of a brilliant candidate for a given prize or position. He will attribute to sheer chance (or to shameful relationship with influential people) the achievements of others. He will silence any positive information regarding others, while amplifying and disseminating the slightest rumor or ambiguous fact that could bring about discredit and criticism on them.

B) ENVY

The first important moment of human life, in the proper sense of the word "human", is the discovery of one's own existence. The conscious experience of the self is our greatest difference with animals, an achievement that is also the origin of considerable psychological work. To begin with, It forces upon us the need to organize our multiple perceptions, ideas and feelings. To do so, we create a value system for deciding that some experiences are more desirable than others, that some things are better and others worse. Eventually, we end up discovering, like Adam and Eve, the science of good and evil.

While we are still in the middle of our first psychological task, we must already take on the second, which starts with the discovery that, in addition to us, there are other people in the world. Hence comes comparative evaluation, the realization of who is big and who is small, of who has power and who has not, of who gives and who receives. The first task eventually becomes the definition and fulcrum of our personal identity; the second leads to the search and eventual happy-fitting into our place within humanity. Both take place early in life, and both require a caring environment and lots of love.

Some people may reach adult age without having made significant advances in any of these two basic tasks. The mind of these immature adults is full of holes, scratches and blots, plagued with terrors and emptiness. It is within this dark terrain that envy takes shape. There is always in the envious person a failure in developing the capacity for gratitude, which may span from the banal to the most malignant.

Gratitude is the affective response to somebody who cares and, in general, for any good received. Gratitude is a feeling close to love, which includes a desire to provide some kind of benefit to the giver. Agratitude is the enjoyment of a good received with no thought or consideration towards the benefactor. This can also be considered normal, as the instances we should be grateful for are so numerous that it is easy to take them for granted. Definitely pathological, however, is ingratitude, a negative affective response for a good received, close to hate, which includes a desire to hurt, damage or injure both the gift and its giver (Klein, 1957) According to the severity of the defect on the capacity for gratitude, we may define three different types of envy.

1. Healthy envy

Envy, one of the capital sins, was defined by St. Thomas as "the sadness felt over somebody's good". The expression "healthy envy" is of common usage in Spanish, although the terms "emulative envy" or "minor self-limited envy" would be more appropriate. This kind of envy is not healthy in itself but is, rather, innocuous. When someone we know or with whom we have some kind of relationship enjoys a feature, feeling, property or achievement that we lack but desire, the first emotional move is of annoyance, a reactive feeling that defines envy. Yet, in a matter of seconds, another feeling arises, a mixture of curiosity, interest and admiration. Incidentally, admiration is the most powerful antidote to all kinds of envy.

> *Get rid of envy. If someone knows, thinks, does or has something that you crave, you must approach him with admiration. And if he allows you to learn how he does it, with gratitude.*

The healthy attitude to envy turns it into a motivational force and corresponds to what Ortega-y-Gasset called the "sporting attitude to life". The existence of people better than us may be annoying, because it forces us to keep working to reach them, but it is also helpful, as they are role models who lead the way on a road that we also want to cover.

2. Competitive envy

This type of envy is characteristic of situations in which the person with superior attributes or possessions is not a model, but an opponent. He is not on our side, but on the opposing team. His gain is our loss. Our suffering over his good is a perfectly logical and reasonable feeling which derives from our concern over the risk of defeat. This type of envy is far from malignant. In many cases, the contenders declare a sincere admiration for each other, without this interfering with their will for defeating the other. The traditional chivalry of the warrior was based on the dissociation between the determination to obtain victory and the assessment of the enemy, who could be admirable and admired. In fields closer to our own experience, we can see this (though not always) between candidates for a scholarship or prize, applicants for a promotion opening, suitors to the same partner and, in general, between competitors who closely share their tastes and desires but who, for objective reasons, can only satisfy them in an exclusive way. The Spanish saying "Courtesy does not exclude courage" may express this feeling.

Special mention must be given to what has been called *just envy*, that is, the indignation felt on observing a benefit obtained by illicit means. If this were truly so, we would not be dealing with envy proper, but with an honest desire to defend justice and decency. Frequently, however, this sort of "just indignation" merely disguises other motives and intentions. Generosity and justice advise one to think twice before casting the first stone. Unleashing the furies of hell over a trifling error or its mere appearance is not necessarily related to a thirst for justice. More often than not, is a sign of malignant envy.

3. Malignant envy

Envy is malignant when the suffering caused by another's good is coupled with enjoyment for his defeat or injury. Therefore, the malignant envious seeks to cause all kinds of harm to his prey, with a dedication that spans from occasional ill-wishes to permanent and obsessive persecution.

Whereas emulation is the principal consequence of healthy envy, predation is that of malignant envy. A person suffering from malignant envy attempts to strip the envied one of everything he considers valuable, not so much for his own benefit, but to prevent and destroy its utility and enjoyment for the other. Quevedo, the famous Spanish satirist, made the incisive observation that "envy is thin, because it bites but does not eat".

In the same way that paranoid delusions grow out of some grain of truth, the fits of envy often begin on some reasonable consideration. It is often observed that the envied person obtains easily some good that the envious can barely approach with the greatest effort. Whoever has seen the *Pink Panther* series of films, in which Peter Sellers brilliantly interpreted the bumbling inspector Clouseau, will recognize this phenomenon in the Superintendent, a methodical man whose sensible projects always fail. In comical contrast, the absurd shenanigans of the clueless Clouseau always achieve the most spectacular success.

Other examples are offered by the story of Snow White and her evil stepmother, who cannot bear being surpassed by Snow White's natural beauty and designs various plots to eliminate her; or by the consuming hate of Salieri, a hard working composer, to the much more gifted and creative Mozart.

Malignant envy is often seen in action in academic circles (Westhues, 2004, 2005). Jauregui (2000), a brilliant anthropologist who suffered harassment to the point of being stripped of his Chair, summarizes the plight of the famous medieval professor Fray Luis de Leon, very much like his own:

The mediocre professors were suffering the painful lashings of envy and designed a dirty strategy to eliminate a great professor from his chair. As the envious person cannot beat the object of his envy by playing fair, as the mediocre professors cannot compete with Fray Luis de Leon either in publications or in teaching, they designed a dirty strategy. .. Knowing they will never be able to reach his brilliance either by writing his poetry or by inspiring students with his wisdom, oratory and passion... these mediocre professors, corroded by envy, design numerous plots to eliminate Fray Luis from the academic stage. They accuse him of being a heretic. With this ploy they manage an initial victory, as the master is removed from his chair and placed behind bars.

C) CONTROL

From a trace of DNA found within a drop of resin, extinct dinosaurs return to life cloned by a group of scientists half greedy, half mad. This is the premise for Michel Crichton´s *Jurassic Park*. The main character is concerned over the potential ecological consequences of the project, but one of the park scientists replies with great confidence, "Don't worry, they can't reproduce". The main character shakes his head and declares: "Life will find its way".

As anyone who has read the novel (or seen the film) will recall, life did find its way. The dinosaurs multiplied and the result was the kind of chaos we can imagine in a world full of prehistoric beasts. The moral of the story is that life is unpredictable and cannot be controlled. Or, rather, that the only thing we can predict about life is that it "will find its way", doing pretty much whatever it pleases.

Erich Fromm, the famous German psychoanalyst who practiced in Mexico, described two personality dynamics that everyone possesses, though one of them always predominates to a greater or lesser extent in each individual. He called one of these *biophilia*, literally "the love of the living", and the other *tanatophilia*, "the love of the dead". A predominance of biophilia helps a person to accept the chaos associated with life, and even to enjoy it. Biophilic people value compassion, empathy, and care more than order, organization, and cleanliness. Tanatophilics, in contrast, prefer the later over the former, and thus like mechanical, rigid, predictable and controllable things. It is not that they are brutal and aggressive assassins, in fact they tend to be quite polite and educated; but inevitably, living beings annoy them, as these tend to disorganize their world.

The most unpredictable and uncontrollable living beings are, by far, the humans. A true tanatophilic cannot bear them. His first reaction is to ignore them, generally by shielding himself behind some kind of machine. But if this technique does not work, he will attempt to control them through the process of *dehumanization*, by which the other person is denied human status. Its opposite is *anthropomorphism*, the common practice of children and primitive peoples of attributing human-like will and intentions to animals and objects. Whereas anthropomorphism increases the complexity of life, dehumanization simplifies life, making it much more controllable by diminishing the number of interacting beings. In its lighter form, dehumanization does not completely negate the other's human condition, but merely his capacity to actively participate in a given situation. In its heaviest form, people are turned into things, devitalized, so that they become simple numbers, material elements of a project, "human resources", unperfected androids.

Dehumanization explains why the harasser is so pitiless. The more helpless and desperate is the victim, the more evident is the efficacy of the harasser control method. On the other hand, the more the victim suffers, the more essential is his dehumanization, in order to stifle any lingering empathic feeling. It is not the same to dismember a doll, something that innocent children may carry out routinely, than to torture a human being; it is not the same to kick a ball than it is to kick someone's behind. To treat a person as a thing is not only to deny him volition and feeling but also to be able to do it without guilt. A subtle form of control is seduction. Seduced men or women believe themselves to be the object of the other's love, but in reality they are no more than an instrument for the satisfaction of pleasure, or of any other desire. Seduction, which is basically deception and betrayal, serves as a means of control because it denies and destroys human identity, reducing the seduced person to a mere utilitarian instrument.

II.- Factors that depend on the victim

The individual marked out for WPH displays a combination of visible talent for his job with the inability to butter up his superiors and to avoid the envy of his peers. This risk has been recognized since ancient times, as is shown by the I Ching sentence "Prince Wen, of noble appearance, sharp intelligence and charming manners, was, *therefore,* in grave danger."

There are three main features that identify individuals at high-risk of harassment. The first is authenticity, understood as commitment to his own inner development without concern for external conveniences; the second is psychological naivety or incapacity to discover the hidden intentions of others; the third is active emotional dependence, a need to be loved and valued for his own efforts and merits.

In certain quarters, the attitude of authenticity provokes distrust and opposition, which the future victim can neither foresee nor prevent due to the second feature of psychological naivety. Even so, he could escape from the most severe harms were it not for his emotional dependence, which causes him to maintain relationships that he should avoid with determination and to seek help from the very same people that are harassing him.

A) AUTHENTICITY

In contrast with those who care about control and predictability, the authentic individual seeks, above all else, self-realization and self-knowledge. When he devotes himself to a task, he does it out of inner conviction, with little consideration for convenience or material rewards. As he is keen to achieve the expression of his potential, he is used to apply himself to the painful task of self-discovery. The most crucial moment of this internal search takes place in late adolescence, when a choice has to be made between the different possible paths of life. "Living the unknown potential" is the feeling that there is a reason for being in this world, even if one does not know exactly what this might be.

The authentic person looks for a "path with heart", a career which feels right, and he commits himself to a destiny which he may know very little about, except that it is his own. Meanwhile, others eschew their potential and settle for any activity that seems comfortable and predictable. In due time, they will turn against those who remained true to their real self. When the biblical Esau sold his birthright for a plate of lentils, he was convinced of getting a good deal. But as soon as he finished eating, he despaired and attempted to kill his brother Jacob. The same thing happens with those who renounce their authenticity for the apparent comfort of material benefits. Eventually desperation gnaws at them, as well as hate towards those who have managed to stay true to their destiny.

B) PSYCHOLOGICAL INNOCENCE

The usual conception of psychological innocence or naivety as a synonym of candor, simplicity and absence of guile does not quite capture the fact that, more than a virtue, it often reveals a defect in the construction of the personality.

The origins of the word innocence can be traced to the Sanskrit term *nek*, "death", from which the latin *nocere*, "to injure" derives. Innocence is the negation of *nek,* the inability of injuring, and by extension, that of perceiving in others the intention to do so. To be innocent or naive is to think that the whole world is good, which, given that evil exists, is an obvious error. In this context, I will define *psychological innocence* as *the relative incapacity to perceive in depth the malevolent intentions of others*. According to its origin, innocence can be natural or reactive, and according to the way it develops, primary or secondary and conscious or unconscious.

Primary natural innocence: precedes the formation of a concept of good and evil, and so is found only in animals, very little children and severely mentally retarded adults

Secondary natural innocence: a chosen innocence, such as that of the saint who, in the face of evil, opts for forgiveness and prefers his destruction to raising his hand against his fellow man.

Conscious reactive innocence: sages (and I do not refer to any mere academic or researcher, but to people of true wisdom and knowledge) usually develop a form of innocence in their efforts to understand the universe. The innocence of the wise man (think of Einstein, Pythagoras, Seneca...) is not chosen like that of the saint, but is a logical and conscious development, proper to the elevated state of understanding he has achieved.

Unconscious reactive (or defensive) innocence: reasonably normal individuals with a high risk of being abused display a curious type of innocence, which leads them through life as if everyone were on their side and there were nothing to fear. Indeed, if they happen to have any merits at all, they tend to succeed quite easily, as it is true that most people have a good heart, and innocence brings out people's sympathy. But it is only a question of time and (bad) luck before the innocent finds himself with an abuser who will make true the Chinese proverb:

"Whoever is dressed as a person of high rank but rides in a poor carriage, invites thieves."

To ride in a poor carriage is to go about unprotected, without taking adequate precautions, which is appropriate for someone who has nothing to lose, but inappropriate for someone who owns valuable goods. The abuser jumps on the innocent victim with the enthusiasm of a highway robber that chances upon a "person of high rank" with no escort.

Saints, sages and mentally retarded persons are at risk of being abused, and they often are. But as their number is proportionally low, and in addition, they tend to benefit from the situation (at least saints), I will not deal with them in any detail. On the other hand, the unconscious defensive innocent merits a great deal of interest, as he represents a large proportion of the general population, and tends to suffer a huge amount of misery as a result of WPH, a destructive experience that may interrupt, sometimes permanently, a promising career. The normal victim of WPH does not choose to return to the state of natural innocence, like the saint, nor does he consciously develop his innocence, like the sage. His intelligence is at least normal, so his problem has to be different from that of the mentally retarded. However, his actions reveal subtle but crucial failures to anticipate consequences, as well as a certain failure to understand other people's motives.

A SPECIAL CASE: WPH
IN THE HEALTH SYSTEM

Though Goleman (1995) does not specifically mention harassment, he does point out that Emotional Intelligence tends to be low in children who are rejected or unpopular at school. On the other hand, Tim Field makes the same suggestion on the reverse, attributing the high levels of harassment within the English Health Service to the preference of individuals at risk for WPH for roles where they can apply their empathic qualities (direct service for patients), while abusers gravitate towards jobs in which they can exert their tanatophilic urges for control (management).

From Tim Field´s classification of health workers into "emphatics" and "controllers", the following line of argument follows:

Empathic aspects of personality, such as sensitivity, comprehension of others and interest towards the development and well-being of others, predominate among doctors, nurses and other caretakers.

Controlling aspects of personality predominate among bureaucrats and management personnel, as these aspects naturally lead the person to avoid a relationship with patients and devote their energies towards control and resource optimization.

Under these conditions, the activities of management can easily degenerate towards abusive relationships, in the extent to which bureaucrats treat patients and doctors as things ("resources" and "targets"), interpreting some empathic actions of caretakers as a challenge or threat towards their institutional power.

PSYCHODYNAMICS OF INNOCENCE

Psychological innocence is an important risk factor, which deserves careful study. The psychotherapeutic treatment of individuals who have suffered WPH has allowed me to develop the hypothesis of *unconscious defensive innocence, a* defense mechanism that explains the apparent contradiction first described in health workers: How can emotionally intelligent and empathic people fail to detect malevolent and envious feelings in others?.

Succinctly summarizing my hypothesis, the individual at risk for WPH is naturally able to understand, even too well, the full range of hidden intentions and feelings, both of the self and of others. However, at some point in his development, a specific traumatic event overloads his ability to integrate contradictions related to affection, initiating a defensive shutdown of his capacity to detect envy. If similar events are repeated with a certain temporal proximity, the functional inhibition crystallizes in a persistent loss of this capacity. This leads to a poor perception of envy and malevolence, a trait systematically found in subjects given to suffer abuse in general and WPH in particular. The process begins early, in an automatic and unconscious manner, and during a critical moment of development, the mechanisms that detect envy are overloaded to such an extent that they lose their functionality, and with it their ability to inform the individual regarding feelings of envy, either of the self or of others. The following case-vignette illustrates the phenomenon:

M. is a thirty-four years old university professor who comes to therapy with symptoms of anxiety and depression. The symptoms arise during a situation of WPH that has lasted several years. Her personal history displays the predictable risk factors of authenticity, naivety and emotional dependence. A specific psychotherapy for WPH-related syndromes is initiated, followed by symptomatic recovery. Her traumatic history, her inability to take best advantage of her evident personal and intellectual potential, the repeated instability of her intimate relationships and the evident reactive character of her psychological innocence suggest that treatment should continue through autogenic analysis. This is an extract from one of the key sessions:

_"My mother is smiling while I cry. I don't understand why she laughs, but I feel evil, really evil, I feel horns and a tail sprouting and I'm turning into a devil. I hate her because she's happy while I suffer, I jump on her and begin to bite her neck, I tear it out in chunks and begin to grow very quickly, I'm bigger than she is now, I grow so big that I break the walls of the room, everything collapses on me, rocks, fire, a volcano is exploding....

Autogenic analysis applies a technique that improves upon Freud's "free association", allowing for a more direct access to the unconscious fantasies created on defense of traumatic feelings. The therapeutic action is related to the activation and maintenance of the process of extraconscious recovery in itself, rather than to the interpretation of the specific content of the fantasies uncovered. But from the theoretical point of view, these meanings are important to establish the basic operative dynamics for different pathologies.

In the case of M., the fragment from this session shows the creation of dynamics around traumatic envy. The discrepancy between the emotional states of mother and daughter is followed by the aggressive taking and incorporating of parts of the mother ("I tear it out in chunks") which enables her to grow, though in an exaggerated and destructive way. The scene ends with the destruction of the daughter herself and of the things enviously incorporated. The fantasy of growing and becoming like the mother reveals a competitive envy that is quite normal, which is complicated by the enormous indiscriminate aggression typical of malignant envy. The initial scene, in which the mother laughs at the daughter, is repeated often in different sessions. Although in autogenic analysis it is always difficult to distinguish between memories and fantasies, the scene corresponds so accurately with the "distant and demanding" way in which M. reports having always been treated by her mother that it very possibly refers to a real traumatic occurrence.

M., very intelligent and attractive since her childhood, felt that she was her father's favorite, and she always kept a very close relationship with him. The patient assures that this did not appear to bother her mother, who, on the contrary, took it quite good-humouredly and occasionally referred to them playfully in public as a "little couple".

Though M. is not aware of it, her entire childhood relationship with her mother seems affected by the envy of the latter towards the former, displayed very subtly. It is possible that even her mother was not conscious of her envy towards her playful and attractive daughter, whom the man of the family paid more attention to than to herself. The smile of the mother before her daughter's tears is a traumatic image that condenses the experience of suffering her mother's envy ("enjoying another's misfortune").

It is also evident that M. did not do anything to appease this envy, but rather that she attempted to stimulate it, appearing to derive a certain pleasure in marginalizing and punishing her mother. This behavior closed an interactive envy circuit that at some points must have become so stressful that it finally disappeared from consciousness. However, as always tends to happen, whatever is repressed eventually surfaces in some way, generally inappropriate and destructive. As an adult, M. was incapable of realizing how she created intense feelings of envy in her boss, a woman with whom she seemed to reproduce certain aspects of her childhood relationship with her mother. As a result, instead of identifying the first premonitory signals and reacting quickly and adequately, she continued to worsen a situation that became ever more harmful.

C) EMOTIONAL DEPENDENCE

Individuals at risk of abuse include, at the core of their personality, a depressive and dependent tendency that makes them vulnerable to the seduction techniques of the typical abuser. On the other hand, these tendencies also allow him to understand and respond positively to other people's needs for affection. For this reason, in general, his emotional relationships tend to be good if other dynamics do not interfere, such as envy or the need to control.

The person at risk for WPH tends to have a better relationship with people at a lower hierarchical level (students, patients, clients and some collaborators), with whom affective exchanges are more important than competitive dynamics, than with people at his own or higher level, in which envy dynamics can predominate.

When an interpersonal relationship has been established, the interpersonal ties seem to take on life, and they certainly are alive from the psychological point of view. A breakdown of these ties is painful, in a manner proportional to the emotional dependence of each individual. The psychopath, at one extreme, conceives himself from early childhood as alone in the world, and, in consequence, considers every relationship in an utilitarian, cold and disposable way. The person at risk for WPH is at the other end of the spectrum. Due to his peculiar manner of adapting to hostile relationships during childhood (which I have defined as *unconscious defensive innocence, with inhibition of envy*), he tends to protect every relationship, lest he will suffer from affective deprivation. Therefore he needs to protect and maintain his interpersonal ties, even if they bind him to a dangerous enemy or to a dead weight that drags him to the depths.

In normal circumstances, the consequences of emotional dependence are not very obvious, as they are limited to a certain hypersensibility to rejection and a moderate tendency towards pathological mourning. But in stressful situations, a number of harmful additional elements may appear:

1 Ceaseless and anxious search for security and support in the immediate social environment, which can lead to rejection.

2 Excessive value on the initial rejection of potential helpers, which may generate an even more stifling search for help, which, in turn, can provoke further resentment of his family and friends. This is unfortunate, as these people would be of great help, if they were not pressured beyond their supportive capacities.

3 Offended by an insufficient answer, and in order to protect himself from greater narcissistic harm, the abused person may give up on his search for help and thus enters a phase of affective withdrawal from his loved ones, precisely when he most needs their care and support.

4 Paradoxically, in WPH the victim may seek help from the abusers themselves, demonstrating not only his psychological

innocence but also his need to recuperate their love and protection.

Emotional dependence explains why the victim does not break off the relationship in cases of abuse within a couple, being able to endure anything in order to maintain bonds that are, in reality, chains of slavery. In cases of institutional abuse or of WPH, this is one of the factors that delay the discovery of the true situation. The profound dissatisfaction with himself in the face of the evidence of not being loved leads the victim of WPH to devise all kinds of explanations and strategies to recover the acceptance of others, unable to recognize that he is being attacked and destroyed by the same people who should protect and encourage him.

III.- Factors that depend on the environment

The abuse that takes place in a
social context, as in the case of institutional
harassment or mobbing, could not occur
without the complicity and permissiveness
of the rest of the organization. The
harassment and persecution in WPH
develops in the midst of a surprising
silence and inhibition of the observers who,
though fully conscious of the abuse and
injustice of the situation, abstain from
intervening, either out of implicit complicity
with the strategy of eliminating the victim,
or to avoid becoming targets of punishment
themselves. It is not rare for ambitious
individuals of scarce professional worth to
take advantage of the situation consciously,

as it benefits them by removing from their path a more qualified competitor.

The three organizational factors that facilitate WPH are the isolation with respect to the rest of the world, the internal cohesion of the group and a general inefficiency or lack of pressure towards production or creativity.

A) ISOLATION

By social isolation, I am referring to a situation in which both input and outputs of information from a wider social structure are minimal or, in any case, not free. The organization filters and selects information, discarding or distorting any data that may be used for questioning or interfering with its usual proceedings. In general, the isolation of a group or organization is self-imposed as part of its functional activity, and unquestionably accepted by all its members. Various internal norms and cultural structures may impede free communication and the spread of information, either to protect the group from contamination with inferior external elements, or merely for defensive reasons, to protect the group from every dissonance that could question or put the internal culture of the institution at risk.

Some strategies that allow organizations to actively generate their own isolation are the following:
-The existence of procedures that favor the admission of new members who are related

previously in some way with internal members (that is, nepotism).

-Specific rules that limit the access of observers, moderators or evaluators external to the institution.

- An institutional culture that rejects foreign interference and seeks to keep agreements, decisions and disagreements "in house".

-Inhibition of internal democracy, either through the lack of appropriate organs, or through the fraudulent manipulation of these organs, situation accepted by the internal culture of the Institution.

The consequence and aim of all these measures is the preservation of an autarchic organization, made up of people whose loyalty is guaranteed, among other things because their isolation limits their capacity to move to an alternative group.

The generalized lack of information facilitates the manipulation of internal opinion, which usually concentrates on self-protection and self-complacency. The discrepancies with external forces or organizations are interpreted as displays of enmity by those forces or organizations, and contribute to further reinforce the isolation and the cohesion of the group. Naturally, worker-unions or similar activities are minimal in such organizations, and if they take place, tend to be corrupt and controlled by the organization itself.

B) COHESION

This factor is a necessary consequence and complement of the previous. Isolation facilitates and forces the union between the members of the organization by limiting the possibility of external ties. Those ties guarantee and define the cohesion of the group, and can be characterized as being irresponsible. An irresponsible relationship is defined as that which is established or maintained by requirements or reasons beyond the will of the individual, over which he has no real responsibility. Irresponsible ties are, to use an ancient term, inalienable, that is, impossible to give up or to question.

Relationships established according to

personal taste or inclination, mutual interest or cooperation towards some goal, have a personal foundation. On the other hand, relationships between members of a cohesive group have an institutional basis, because they derive their power from an "institutional principle" that is deemed superior to personal responsibility, preference or convenience. This cohesive institutional principle on a superior level is what The Godfather calls *la famiglia* and rats call *the smell of the clan.* Members of the cohesive group recognize each other through identification with this principle, a state known as "*being one of us*".

Any attempt, observed or suspected, of emancipating, distancing or escaping from the group is understood as a betrayal of the institutional dynamic and therefore persecuted. For this reason, high rates of abuse have been found within regimented and homogeneous institutions such as schools, armed forces and, in general, conservative institutions where strong ties and identities are shared among members and there is little tolerance for diversity. For someone who is not "one of us", *the smell of the clan stinks*, and the mere presence of such a person within the organization represents an insult for all the rest.

C) LACK OF PRODUCTIVITY

The occurrence of WPH is more likely within organizations whose internal culture values power and control over productivity and efficiency. For this reason, it seems to happen more frequently within universities, hospitals and NGO's, though no public or private entity can escape the problem. However, businesses that must finance themselves to survive cannot afford the waste of energy, time, emotions, and intelligence required to maintain situations of harassment, nor can they lose or stifle valuable members. If the company is large enough or obtains sufficient funds from outside sources, it may survive for a long period despite major economic losses and disastrous balance sheets as well as, from the point of view of its human capital, a quick turnover (entry and exit of professionals who stay in the organization for only a brief period), high levels of absenteeism and prolonged sick leaves.

It is also common to find within these organizations a high degree of legal conflict, particularly over labor issues, with frequent court decisions against the organizations and huge compensations being paid out. The external application of any measure of productivity or, more simply, the demand that the organization produce anything at all, is received as an insult by its management team, who prefers bankruptcy and closure before changing internal power structures.

Conclusion

Psychological abuse in its institutional form is an extended situation of destructive persecution within an organization, initiated and maintained due to three factors: the personality of the victim, the personality of the abuser, and the characteristics of the organization itself.

The defining characteristics of the abuser include the need for control, envy and a poor capacity for appreciating and stimulating excellence; those of the victim include a primary focus on his own authenticity, a certain incapacity for perceiving and managing envy from the others and the need to be loved and appreciated. Albeit those qualities may be endearing for sane people, all of them are despicable for the abuser, who perceives:

-authenticity as disrespect for authority, lack of interest towards the group and a tendency to do his own thing,

-psychological innocence as an arrogant and insolent attitude that has no respect for the intentions and status of others

-emotional dependence as a weakness to be exploited as a first point of attack.

The person at risk for WPH, engaged in his own work and personal development, has no particular stance towards the abuser, and feels confused and surprised when the harassment begins. In his attempts to understand and clear up the situation he commits all the mistakes necessary to make it even worse, and, as a result, develops a psychological reaction of stress with symptoms of anxiety, depression and somatization.

Keeping in mind the huge discrepancies between their personalities and attitudes to life, it is clear that the hate of the abuser towards his victim is unavoidable and predictable.

The distaste and disinterest of the victim towards his abuser is also predictable, but it would not be inevitable if he realized that his own authenticity and

85

functional blindness to envy reduce his ability to perceive and prevent the attack which he is about to suffer.

A specular case of the abuse-risk person, the exact contrary, is the ambitious character interested only in his own personal career at all costs. His great ability to understand power and envy dynamics and to use them to his own advantage allows him to become the sidekick of the abuser, and, more often than not, also the ideal substitute of the abuse victim.

The key catalyst in sparking up and developing the abuse relationship is the rest of the organization. Without the participation of this "third factor", the abuse could not take place, nor could the abuser reach decision-making positions, nor could the ambitious careerist climb up the corporate ladder.

A free and democratic organization that has not been spoiled by isolation, irresponsible cohesion and ineffectiveness will not allow the persecution of someone who deserves to be considered a valuable and important member. Nevertheless, if the organization changes, the person at risk of abuse becomes a victim of abuse, and his official standing drops quickly, surprisingly and unexplainably. Those who used to be his friends and admirers now avoid him, partly out of fear, and partly because they hope to climb up the ladder space he has freed up. The transformation can be slow and subterranean or lightning fast. Some organizations keep a double culture, swaying quickly from high consideration to a brilliant and hardworking authentic, naïve, emotional-dependent individual (thus, at risk for WPH) to his relentless persecution, depending on the changes taking place in the upper echelons.

As a final thought, it is worth keeping in mind that, as ethological studies demonstrate, the mobbing tendency is a part of nature. As an example, Lorenz´s experiments show that rats from the same pack share a common odor, and they recognize each other for it. If a new rat is introduced in a long standing pack, the other rats will smell it, and then attack it furiously to the death as soon as they discover its lack of the appropriate stench. The more an institution resembles rat society, the more probable it is that WPH will flourish within its core. It is a task of human effort to transform its groups and businesses into organizations that foster the development, creativity and well-being of its members, and not just their allegiance to the "status quo" and the institutionalization of authority.

APENDIX

Psychopathological effects of Work Place Harassment.

By Luis de Rivera, MD, FRCP(C),

and Manuel Rodriguez-Abuin, PhD

Institute of Psychotherapy and

Psychosomatic Research, Madrid, Spain

Scientific and Clinical Report nº 39 — Session 13.

Violence, Trauma and Victimization. Syllabus and

Proceedings Summary p. 85.

American Psychiatric Association 159th. Annual

Meeting, Toronto, 2006.

ABSTRACT

194 subjects (72 males and 122 females)

complaining of Work Place Harassment

(WPH) were evaluated with the Spanish

version of Derogatis´ 90 symptoms Check-

91

List Revised (SCL 90 R). A group of 311 neurotic ambulatory psychiatric patients of similar demographic characteristics were used as a comparison group. The harassed workers had significant higher scores than the mixed neurotic sample in the Total of Positive symptoms (PST) and in the symptom dimensions of paranoid ideation, obsession-compulsion, hostility and depression.

Those with lower job status had higher General Symptom Index than those with medium-high job status. Women had higher somatisation index than men. There were no significant differences related to marital status.

Method

We applied the Spanish version of Derogatis' SCL9OR questionnaire (de Rivera, 2002) to 194 consecutive complainants registered by the Spanish Association against Psychological Harassment at the Workplace. All the subjects had been previously tested with the LIPT-60 (Spanish version of the Leymann Inventory of Psychological Terrorization — 60 items) (de Rivera, 2005) and interviewed by psychological trained officers of the Association, who excluded those who did not fit our operational definition of mobbing by five criteria (see page 11, above). Of the 194 subjects, 72 were males and 122 females. The mean of age was 43 (SD = 10), with a range from 18 to 67. As for the job status, we classified 91 as low-medium (clerical, blue collar, unqualified workers...) and 103 as medium-high (professionals, specialists, executives...). We compared the measurements obtained in the SCL9OR with the normalised values found in the general population and in ambulatory psychiatric patients in Spain, described in our Spanish version of SCL9OR. For statistical analysis we applied the SPSS-13 to perform the two-tailed Student test for two samples.

Results

The general scores and all the dimensions of psychopathology were significantly higher in the harassed workers than in the general population. In addition, the scores for the dimensions of Paranoid Ideation, Hostility,

Depression and Obsession-compulsion were significantly higher in the harassed workers than in the sample of ambulatory psychiatric patients (table 1). Comparison by sex in the harassed workers sample show higher scores for somatisation in females (mean score 1.74 s.d. 0.97 vs mean score 1.35 s.d. 0.85 in males; $p<0.01$), with no significant differences in the remaining symptomatic dimensions. When compared by job level, those with lower job status scored significantly higher in all general indexes of distress (GSI = 1.74 s.d. 0.75 vs 1.44 sd 0.74; PST= 63, s.d. 17.95 vs 56.41, s.d. 19.69; PSDI = 2.38, sd 0.61 vs 2.18, sd 0.6) and in the symptomatic dimensions of somatisation (1.86 sd 0.95 vs 1.37 sd 0.85), obsessionality (1.99 sd 0.92 vs 1.66, sd

0.91), anxiety (1.87 sd 0.93 vs 1.57 sd 0.9) and phobic anxiety (1.18 sd 0.92 vs 0.71 sd 0.93) . There were no significant differences related to marital status, albeit there is a definite trend to more psychopathology in widowed and separated workers.

Discussion

Our findings confirm the widespread observation that mobbing, adult bullying or, as we prefer to term it, work place harassment, is related to the production of severe psychopathology. The characteristic symptoms profile clearly differentiates this population from the bulk of ambulatory psychiatric patients, mostly neurotics with mixed anxiety / depression symptoms.

There is, however, a point of caution in the interpretation of our results: The high scores in paranoidism and hostility may reflect a previous tendency to misinterpret and to overreact to environmental cues. On the other hand, the structure of the psychometric instrument applied is such that whoever feels mistreated and persecuted will rate highly in paranoidism, regardless of the degree in which those feelings are grounded on reality. Longitudinal studies are needed to further elucidate the cause-effect relationship of this finding. In our clinical experience, the hostile-paranoid evolution is a frequent aftermath of WPH, rather than a precedent.

The lack of significant differences related to marital status may be due to the insufficient size of our sample to illustrate the effect of marital status. The definite trend to more psychopathology in widowed and separated workers makes sense in view of the current concepts on the protective effects of social support. Unfortunately, our sample is not big enough to discard that those differences are due to chance.

The higher levels of psychopathology found in workers in lower status jobs are in agreement with the worse self-perceived health status and physical symptoms found by Marmott et al (1991) in subjects in lower status jobs

Table 1. Dimensions of psychopathology in victims of WPH, normal population and ambulatory psychiatric patients.

	WPH subjects (n= 194)	Ambulatory Psychiatric (n= 303)	General population (n= 530)
	Mean and sd	Mean and sd	Mean and sd
SOM	1, 60 (0,94)	1,53 (0,97)	0,56 (0,55)**
OBS	1,88 (0,93)	1,64 (0,99) **	0,60 (0,51)**
INT S	1,49 (0,85)	1,40 (0,96)	0,46 (0,44)**
DEP	2,06 (0,96)	1,88 (0,95)*	0,72 (0,55)**
ANX	1,73 (0,94)	1,61 (0,99)	0,51 (0,48)**
HOST	1,42 (1,07)	1,16 (1,01)**	0,46 (0,53)**
FOB	0,92 (0,96)	1,01 (1,02)	0,25 (0,37)**
PAR	1,67 (0,93)	1,30 (0,98)**	0,47(0,50)**
PSY	0,99(0,76)	1,02 (0,88)	0,22(0,30)**
GSI	1,59 (0,77)	1,47 (0,80)	0,51 (0,36)**
PST	59,43 (19,28)	52,79 (19,77)**	25,32 (14,30)**
PSDI	2,29 (0,61)	2,35 (0,65)	1,73 (0,48)**

* P<0·05
** P<0·01
(In relation to the sample of harassed subjects)

Table 2. Psychopathology by job level

	LOW-MEDIUM (n= 91) Mean and sd	MEDIUM-HIGH (n=103) Mean and sd
SOM **	1·86 (0·95)	1·37 (0·85)
OBS*	1·99 (0·92)	1·66 (0·91)
INT S	1·57 (1·42)	1·42 (0·81)
DEP	2·15 (0·91)	1·94 (1·01)
ANX*	1·87 (0·93)	1·57(0·90)
HOST	1·54 (1·06)	1·25 (1·01)
FOB**	1·18 (0·92)	0·71 (0·93)
PAR	1·79 (0·92)	1·61 (0·88)
PSY	1·1 (0·78)	0·88 (0·71)
GSI*	1·74 (0·75)	1·44 (0·74)
PST*	63 (17·95)	56·41 (19·69)
PSDI*	2·38 (0·61)	2·18 (0·60)

* P<0·05
** P<0·01

Table 3. Psychopathology by sex´

	MALES (n=72) Mean and sd	FEMALES (n=122) Mean and sd
SOM **	1,35 (0,85)	1,74 (0,97)
OBS	1,89 (0,92)	1,88 (0,93)
INT S	1,47 (0,87)	1,51 (0,84)
DEP	1,98 (0,98)	2,11 (0,95)
ANX	1,65 (0,93)	1,78 (0,94)
HOST	1,44 (1,12)	1,41 (1,04)
FOB	0,84 (1,04)	0,97 (0,91)
PAR	1,51 (0,91)	1,77(0,92)
PSY	0,97(0,83)	1 (0,71)
GSI	1,53 (0,77)	1,64 (0,78)
PST	59,12 (18,48)	59,60 (19,82)
PSDI	2,21 (0,63)	2,35 (0,59)

* P<0·05
** P<0·01

REFERENCES

Brodsky, CM: The Harassed Worker. Lexinton, Mass, 1976

Cusack, S Workplace bullying: icebergs in sight, soundings needed. The Lancet, (2000): 356:2118

de Rivera, Luis. El Trastorno por Mediocridad Inoperante Activa (síndrome MIA) Psiquis, 1997, 18 (6): 229-231

de Rivera, Luis. El Maltrato Psicológico. Como defenderse del bullying, el mobbing y otras formas de acoso. Madrid, Espasa-Calpe, 2002

de Rivera, Luis: Creativity and Psychosis in Scientific Research. The American journal of Psychoanalysis 1993, 53:77-84

de Rivera, Luis G, De las Cuevas C,
Rodríguez-Abuin M, Rodríguez Pulido F.
El Cuestionario de Noventa Síntomas
(Adaptación española del Symptom
Check List de Derogatis, SCL-90). T.E.A.
Ediciones, Madrid, 2002.

de Rivera, Luis y Rodríguez-Abuin, MJ:
LIPT-60. Cuestionario de Estrategias de
Acoso en Trabajo. Madrid, EOS. 2005

de Rivera, Luis y Rodríguez-Abuin, M.J. .
Bullying breeds paranoia. British Journal
of Psychiatry 2005
http://bjp.rcpsych.org/cgi/eletters/184/
4/352#764,

de Rivera, Luis: Las Claves del Mobbing.
EOS, Madrid, 2005 p.19

de Rivera, Luis de: Crisis Emocionales.
IPM - CreativeSpace, 2012 –

http://www.amazon.com/Crisis-Emocionales-airosos-reforzados-nuestras/dp/147819734X

European Foundation for the Improvement of Working and Living Conditions. Violence, bullying and harassment in the workplace (2005). Dublin. www.eurofound.eu.int

Field, T. Bully in Sight. How to predict, resist, challenge and combat workplace bullying. Success Unlimited, Wantage, UK, 1996

Goleman, D. Emotional Intelligenca. Bantam, New York, 1995

Hirigoyen, MF. Le Harcelement Moral. Syros, Paris, 1998

Fox, S and Spector, P.E.
Counterproductive Work Behavior.
American Psychological Association,
Washington, 2005

Fromm, E. The Anatomy of Human
Destructiveness. Fawcett Crest Books,
1975

Jáuregui, J.A. Aprender a pensar con
libertad, Martinez Roca, Barcelona 2000,
pg.276.

Klein, Melanie: Envy and Gratitude.
Hogarth Press, 1957

Lester, G, Wilson, B, Griffin, L and
Mullen, PE (2004): Unusually persistent
complainants. British Journal of
Psychiatry, 184 , 352- 356

Leymann, H and Gustafsson, A: Mobbing
at work and the development of

postraumatic stress disorders. (1996).
European Journal of Work and
Organizational Psychology, 5:251-275

Marmot MG, Smith GD, Stansfeld S,
Patel C, North F, Head J, White I,
Brunner E, Feeney A. (1991). Health
inequalities among British civil servants:
the Whitehall II study. The Lancet, 337:
1387-1393.

Maslow, AH: Motivation and Personality.
Harper and Brothers, New York, 1954

McAvoy, BR and Murtagh, J (2003):
Workplace bullying. The silent epidemic
BMJ ; 326:776-777

Mikkelsen, EG and Einarsen, S (2002):
Basic ssumptions and symptoms of post-
traumatic stress among victims of bullying
at work. European Journal of Work and

Organizational Psychology, 11: 87-111

Peck, M.S.   People of the Lie. Arrow
Books, London, 1990

Quine, L : Workplace Bullying in NHS
community trust: staff questionnaire
survey. BMJ, 318:228-232 , 1999

Westhues, K Administrative mobbing at
the University of Toronto. Queenston,
Ontario, The Edwin Mellen Press, 2004

Westhues, K : Workplace Mobbing in
Academia. Queenston, Ontario, The
Edwin Mellen Press, 2004

Westhues, K (Ed.) Winning, losing,
moving on. How professionals deal with
workplace harassment and mobbing.
Queenston, Ontario, The Edwin Mellen
Press, 2005

www.ingramcontent.com/pod-product-compliance
Lightning Source LLC
Chambersburg PA
CBHW072318290526
45794CB00002B/700